THE GREAT™
AMERICAN
HISTORY
QUIZ

Modern Marvels

THE GREAT™
AMERICAN
HISTORY
QUIZ

Modern Marvels

Series Created by
Abbe Raven and Dana Calderwood

Written by
**Charles Norlander, Howard Blumenthal
and Dana Calderwood**

WARNER BOOKS

A Time Warner Company

Copyright ©2000 by A&E Television.
The History Channel, the "H" logo and the Great American History Quiz are trademarks of A&E Television and are registered in the United States and other countries. All Rights Reserved.

Warner Books, Inc., 1271 Avenue of the Americas,
New York, NY 10020

Visit our Web site at www.twbookmark.com

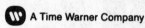 A Time Warner Company

Printed in the United States of America

First Printing: August 2000
10 9 8 7 6 5 4 3 2 1

Library of Congress Cataloging-in-Publication Data

The great American history quiz. Modern Marvels / by the History Channel.
  p.   cm.
  ISBN 0-446-67685-3
  1. Technology—United States—History—Miscellanea.
  2. Inventions—United States—History—Miscellanea   I. History Channel (Television network)
  T21.G74   2000
  609.73—dc21   00-031757

Cover design by Carolyn Lechter
Cover photograph by AP/Wide World Photos
Book design and text composition by Ralph Fowler

This edition of the quiz is called "Modern Marvels." It's the history of great ideas, innovations, and inventions great and small.

What are modern marvels? Well, in today's world, it might be a tiny cell phone. But about seventy years ago, the greatest thing since sliced bread was . . . well, it actually was sliced bread, which had just hit the market.

Back in the 1800s, people marveled at life-changing inventions like electric lights, the telephone . . . and who can forget the excitement that greeted the spatula?

But for us, nothing says "modern marvel" like gigantic marvels of engineering. So away we go. . . .

 At the start of the new millennium, what's the tallest building in the U.S.?

(a) John Hancock Center

(b) One World Trade Center

(c) Sears Tower

A N S W E R

The answer is **(c)**. Chicago's Sears Tower has been the tallest building in the U.S. since 1973. Meanwhile, the Empire State Building has slipped to fourth place among America's skyscrapers.

2 When Hoover Dam plugged up the Colorado River, it created 115 miles of Lake Mead, one of the single largest man-made reservoirs in the entire world. But how big is Hoover Dam itself? If you compared Hoover Dam's length with the Empire State Building's height, whose marvel would be mightier?

(a) Empire State Building

(b) Hoover Dam

A N S W E R

The winner and still champion is **(a)**. The Empire State Building wins the "Whose is bigger?" contest by around six feet. And that's not counting the big guy's 222-foot antenna. But let's face it—the Empire State Building would make a lousy dam.

Although it may no longer be the world's tallest building, the Empire State Building is certainly one of the world's most famous skyscrapers. So here are a few questions about King Kong's favorite New York City landmark.

3 It's quite appropriate that work on one of the world's most celebrated buildings began on a national holiday in 1930. On what holiday did construction begin on the Empire State Building?

(a) Mother's Day

(b) Christmas Eve

(c) St. Patrick's Day

(d) Valentine's Day

ANSWER

(c) The actual construction of the Empire State Building began on St. Patrick's Day, 1930. The luck of the Irish must have been with the construction crew, since the building rose virtually without a hitch—and was completed just over a year later on May 1, 1931.

4 What famous New York politician became the spokesperson for the Empire State Building?

(a) Alfred E. Smith

(b) Franklin Delano Roosevelt

(c) Fiorello LaGuardia

(d) James "Jimmy" Walker

4

A N S W E R

(a) After his unsuccessful presidential bid, Alfred E. Smith was appointed the spokesperson for the Empire State Building.

5 True or false: The antenna on top of the Empire State Building was once used to moor dirigibles.

A N S W E R

True! In a (laughable) effort to beat the Chrysler Building's claim to being the World's Tallest Skyscraper, the owners of the Empire State Building decided to add a 200-foot dirigible (a really fun way to say "airship") mooring mast to the top of the building. Though only one dirigible ever docked at the Empire State Building (for a total of three minutes), the mooring mast gave the Empire State Building the title World's Tallest Building until One World Trade Center was erected in 1972.

6 True or false: A B-2 bomber once crashed into the Empire State Building.

6

A N S W E R

True: On July 28, 1945, a B-2 bomber crashed into the seventy-eighth floor of the Empire State Building, killing fourteen people.

Although most New Yorkers would be loath to admit it, the Empire State Building is no longer the world's tallest building. What building holds that claim to fame?

(a) The Sears Tower, Chicago

(b) The World Trade Center, New York City

(c) The Petronas Towers, Kuala Lumpur, Malaysia

(d) Jin Mao Building, Shanghai, China

7

A N S W E R

(c) Although it's still a title that's hotly contested, the Petronas Towers in Kuala Lumpur is currently regarded as the world's tallest structure, at 1,483 feet.

Clearly, Americans like to be the biggest and the best. Here are two questions about the Mall of America in Bloomington, Minnesota, the largest indoor shopping mall in the U.S., which covers 4.2 million square feet!

 Just how big *is* the Mall of America? If the Statue of Liberty were lying down, how many of her could fit inside the Mall of America?

(a) 50

(b) 142

(c) 258

(d) 301

8

(c) You could fit 258 Statues of Liberty inside the Mall of America. Incidentally, 67 Washington Monuments, 32 Boeing 747s, and 24,336 school buses could also fit inside America's biggest mall.

If you spent ten minutes browsing at every store in the Mall of America, how long would it take you to go through the mall?

(a) 24 hours

(b) 49 hours

(c) 67 hours

(d) 86 hours

ANSWER

(d) You would have to spend 86 hours to cover each of the stores in the Mall of America.

10 What name is given to the 630-foot stainless steel arch on the riverfront in St. Louis?

(a) The Freedom of St. Louis

(b) The Gateway Arch

(c) The Monroe Arch

(d) Missouri's Pride

ANSWER

(b) The Gateway Arch.

11 Which famous Washington, D.C., memorial was designed by a twenty-one-year-old architecture student?

(a) The Vietnam Veteran's Memorial

(b) The Korean War Memorial

(c) The Lincoln Memorial

(d) The Washington Monument

11

ANSWER

(a) Maya Ling Yin was only twenty-one when her design for the Vietnam memorial was selected from over 1,400 different entries.

12 What is the name of the statue that stands on top of the U.S. Capitol in Washington, D.C.?

(a) The Statue of Liberty

(b) Lady Washington

(c) The Statue of America

(d) The Statue of Freedom

12

(d) The Statue of Freedom is perched on top of the Capitol's dome. She is 19'6" tall, and weighs a whopping 15,000 pounds.

13 It took 467 cement trucks an entire day to pour the cement required for the foundation for this famous landmark, built for the 1962 World's Fair. Which landmark is it?

(a) The Perisphere

(b) The Seattle Space Needle

(c) The Chicago Skyride

(d) The Museum of the Americas

13

(b) The Seattle Space Needle.

★ ★ ★ ★ ★ ★ ★ ★

14 Another crucial Modern Marvel debuted at a World's Fair—the 1854 World's Fair, to be exact. This one was responsible for making structures like the Empire State Building, the Eiffel Tower, and the World Trade Center possible. What Modern Marvel is this?

(a) Wrought-iron beams

(b) The elevator

(c) The power drill

(d) Concrete

ANSWER

(b) Elijah Otis, at the request of famed promoter P. T. Barnum, introduced the elevator to the general public at the 1854 World's Fair. Many consider the introduction of the elevator crucial to the development of modern skyscrapers, and they're probably right. Would you want to climb up 103 flights of stairs to work every morning?

★ ★ ★ ★ ★ ★ ★ ★

15 The world's largest post office building is in what U.S. city?

(a) New York

(b) Los Angeles

(c) Chicago

(d) Philadelphia

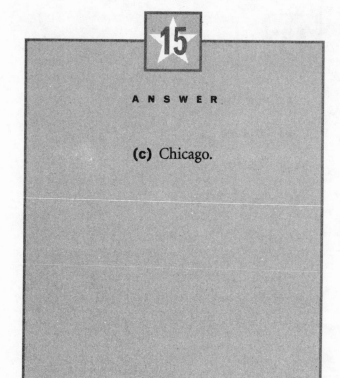

15

ANSWER

(c) Chicago.

Viva Las Vegas! Here are a few brain twisters about Las Vegas, Nevada—a city of Modern Marvels if there ever was one.

 How much money is wagered each year in the world's most famous casino town?

(a) $250 million

(b) $1 billion

(c) $3.5 billion

(d) $5 billion

16

(d) Each year, $5 billion is wagered in Las Vegas. That's greater than the gross national product of about 54 percent of the world's countries. Las Vegas or bust, indeed.

17 Gangster Benjamin "Bugsy" Siegel is often noted as the man who got Las Vegas off the ground. He was the first to build an elegant hotel/casino, where people could go to eat, gamble, and be entertained. What was the name of this Las Vegas landmark?

(a) The Flamingo

(b) The Dunes

(c) Casino Royale

(d) Sands

17

A N S W E R

(a) The Flamingo was Bugsy Siegel's brain-child. He was so concerned about the rest of Las Vegas's underworld that he had his personal suite outfitted with secret passageways, emergency exits, and bullet-proof rooms. Unfortunately, these precautions weren't enough; Bugsy was assassinated in 1947.

18 Not surprisingly, the largest hotel in the world is located in Las Vegas, Nevada. What hotel holds this claim to fame?

(a) The Excalibur

(b) Caesar's

(c) The Tropicana

(d) The MGM Grand

18

(d) With 5,005 rooms the MGM Grand is the largest hotel in the world. If you combined the MGM Grand with the Tropicana and the Excalibur, its closest neighbors, you'd have a hotel with more rooms for rent than are available in the entire city of San Francisco.

True or false: The world's largest pyramid is in Las Vegas.

19

Believe it or not, this is true! The Luxor Hotel, modeled after the Great Pyramid in Egypt, is the world's largest pyramid. The pyramid reaches 350 feet into the sky and is 36 stories tall. The hotel itself has 4,407 rooms, making it the third largest hotel in the world. The beacon on top of the Luxor scores another modern marvel point: It is the brightest beam in the world. The light is so bright that you can use its light to read a newspaper 10 miles out in space.

Not all of our country's really big objects have been marvels of steel and concrete. For example, there's this really big statue in the center of our country. . . .

20 How long does it take to carve a mountain into the world's largest sculpture? Over fifty years so far, and maybe fifty more to complete it! In 1948, sculptor Korczak Ziolkowski began carving a massive Native American on horseback in the Black Hills of South Dakota. Name the great Oglala Lakota leader who is honored by this monument.

(a) Geronimo

(b) Sitting Bull

(c) Crazy Horse

20

(c) Crazy Horse. Unfortunately, Korczak Ziolkowski died in 1982, but his family is continuing his work, determined to finish the monument. In 1998, the completed face of Crazy Horse was unveiled.

21 Here's a question about another famous sculpture: Which of the following presidents is *not* featured on Mt. Rushmore?

(a) Thomas Jefferson

(b) Theodore Roosevelt

(c) Franklin Roosevelt

(d) Abraham Lincoln

21

ANSWER

(c) Franklin Roosevelt is the only president listed who quite literally did not make the cut.

What's faster—the speed of light or the speed of thought? It's probably a close race. And maybe that's why some people who think really fast are called "bright." How bright are you? We'll find out, because it's time for you to think really really fast....

22 The time: Autumn 1997. The place: Nevada's Black Rock Desert. The event: the ultimate car race, pitting speed legend Craig Breedlove against British competitor Andy Green. Breedlove was the master at setting land-speed records, the first human to reach 400, 500, and 600 miles per hour in his jet-powered car called *Spirit of America*. But now he and Andy Green were attempting to raise the record to an unbelievable level. What speed barrier did they intend to break in their cars?

(a) Escape velocity

(b) 1,000 miles per hour

(c) The speed of sound

22

(c) The two men were trying to break the speed of sound. Incredibly, on October 15, 1997, Andy Green did just that. He set a new land-speed record of 763 miles per hour.

23 What's the baddest-looking, fastest-flying plane on the planet? The answer is the SR-71 spy plane, alias the Blackbird. In terms of pure speed, the Blackbird eats Stealth fighters and B-2 bombers for lunch. It's literally quicker than a bullet, 50 percent faster than a Concorde jet, and set a record flying from L.A. to Washington, D.C., in 68 minutes flat. Average speed for that flight: over 2,112 miles per hour. Your question: When did the U.S. military first put the Blackbird into service?

(a) 1968—during the Vietnam War

(b) 1983—during the Grenada invasion

(c) 1991—during the Gulf War

23

(a) 1968. Amazingly, the world's fastest production plane has held that title for more than 30 years. During that time, more than a thousand anti-aircraft missiles have been launched against the Blackbird, but not one has ever caught its target.

24 You've probably heard the term "warp speed." According to the *Star Trek Encyclopedia*, warp factor 1 is equivalent to the speed of light. While NASA hasn't developed anything quite that fast, in 1995 it sent a probe into space that traveled faster than any man-made object ever had before. At the end of a six-year voyage this craft plunged into Jupiter's atmosphere at an astonishing 29 miles per second. What was the name of the spacecraft and probe that made the journey to Jupiter?

(a) *Copernicus*

(b) *Galileo*

(c) *Voyager*

24

(b) *Galileo*, named for the Italian scientist who discovered the major moons of Jupiter. While making its speedy trip, the *Galileo* probe gathered important information about Jupiter's atmosphere.

25 The Brooklyn Bridge: truly one of America's Modern Marvels. Imagine yourself in the growing city of Brooklyn in 1876: tree-lined streets, and nothing taller than your three-story apartment building, except maybe a church steeple. Now here come John and Washington Roebling—a father and son—who build their amazing Brooklyn Bridge to New York City. The bridge's towers soar to thrilling heights, becoming two of the tallest structures in North America. And the main span of the bridge is the longest in the world. One key to this engineering marvel is the metal John Roebling chose to make the cables, a remarkable first that revolutionized suspension bridges. Which metal did Roebling choose?

(a) Iron

(b) Steel

(c) Copper

25

(b) Steel offered greater strength than traditional iron cables, and the suppleness needed to support longer spans. Steel cables have been the choice for suspension bridges ever since the completion of the Brooklyn Bridge.

26 Once the bridge's towers were finished, and while work on its cables continued, Brooklynites wanted to experience their marvelous new bridge, even though its roadway hadn't been built. For the finest view, where did they stroll?

(a) Along a track used to transport supplies

(b) Along the suspension cables

(c) Along a flimsy wooden footbridge

26

(c) A flimsy footbridge, built for workers, was strung between the towers. One popular way to spend a sunny afternoon was a walk high above the East River—with no roadway below! That dangerous route was later closed, but the bridge's permanent center walkway is now one of New York City's finest attractions.

27 The great bridge was an astonishing achievement, spanning a third of a mile across the waters of the East River. This was possible because the towers were built on caissons, gigantic wooden boxes filled with compressed air, each weighing some 3,000 tons. But the caissons proved disastrous for the men who worked inside them. Why?

(a) A caisson collapsed on the workers

(b) The caissons caused a dreaded disease

(c) Workers drowned when water filled a caisson

27

(b) Hundreds of workers suffered the painful and crippling "caisson disease," also called "the bends." It was caused by rapid decompression—workers moved too quickly from the high air pressure inside the caissons to the lower, normal air pressure outside. Even Washington Roebling was stricken, and his wife, Emily, oversaw the completion of the bridge.

The Wright brothers built and piloted the first successful airplane in the world in 1903, but what else do we really know about Orville and Wilbur Wright? We'll provide you with a biographical fact about the Wright brothers, and you must decide whether it's **WRIGHT** or **WRONG**.

28 The Wright brothers' first successful flight was soon followed by wide acclaim for their achievement. Is that fact WRIGHT or WRONG?

28

ANSWER

That's WRONG: Three to four years after their flight took place, most people didn't even believe that their airplane had flown at all.

29 Try this one: One of the students at the Wright brothers' flying school went on to command the U.S. Air Force. Is that WRIGHT or WRONG?

29

ANSWER

The answer is WRIGHT. His name was Henry "Hap" Arnold, and he commanded the U.S. Air Force during World War II. Hap was one of the Wright brothers' students.

30 Okay, here's the next question. Orville had a long feud with the Smithsonian Institution, which claimed one of their officials had built the first "capable" airplane. Is this fact WRIGHT or WRONG?

30

A N S W E R

It's WRIGHT: Orville was so angry, he lent his famous airplane to the Science Museum in London. The Smithsonian finally apologized thirty-nine years later, in 1942, and later got the Wright brothers' plane back.

Now here's another question: No passengers were ever killed during Orville's test flights—is that WRIGHT or WRONG?

31

A N S W E R

WRONG! This is unfortunate, but on one of the test flights, Orville crashed the airplane. Orville was the pilot, and he was seriously injured. His passenger, Lieutenant Thomas Selfridge, was actually the first person ever killed in an airplane accident.

32 Okay, now the last question: Although Orville and Wilbur are the famous brothers, there were actually five Wright

brothers in all. Is that WRIGHT or WRONG?

32

It's WRIGHT. There were five Wright brothers: Orville, Wilbur, Reuchlin, Lorin, and Otis.

Before the Civil War, railroads were pretty much a regional affair, but the dream was to build a railroad from one coast to the other. Here are a few questions about trains and locomotives.

33 On May 10, 1869, U.S. rail travel changed forever. That's when the Union Pacific and Central Pacific met up to complete the first transcontinental railroad. With the new coast-to-coast tracks, travel time for crossing the country was cut from months to days. Excitement about the railroad ran so high that both the final spike and sledgehammer were wired to telegraphically send the sound across the nation. But this didn't work as planned, so the telegraph operator simply clicked a one-word message: "Done." The question is: Where was the railroad finally connected?

(a) Ohio

(b) Utah

(c) Kansas

33

(b) It was in Promontory, Utah. Despite popular legend, the final spike that completed the track was made of iron, not gold. But four "ceremonial" spikes were also driven that day, and two of them were gold.

34 Trains revolutionized not only the way Americans travel, but also the way we tell time. Before trains, each town actually set its own local time! This was a nightmare for railroads as they connected the country and tried to establish schedules. Passengers crossing the U.S. might change their watches dozens of times to make connections. To solve this mess, the railroads and government finally got together and created our four national time zones. The question is: What year did that happen?

(a) 1823

(b) 1853

(c) 1883

34

(c) 1883. Standard time zones made rail travel much more predictable, and our wired world would be impossible without them. Just imagine your TV schedule: "Watch *The Great American History Quiz*™ tonight at 8 o'clock New York time, 7:39 Philadelphia time, 6:44 Toledo time, 4:17 Denver time . . ." Oh, why not just read this book instead?

35 . . . And then the trains went underground: The first American subway system was opened in this city in 1897.

(a) New York

(b) Boston

(c) Washington, D. C.

(d) Baltimore

35

(b) The famous Boston T is the oldest subway line in the country.

Sometimes, when corporate America releases a new Modern Marvel, we, the people, respond with a raspberry. The Edsel was Ford's fabulous failure—and the car's name has come to represent products that nobody wants to buy. So we proudly present . . . the Edsel Awards, or: "Products That Got a Lot of People Fired."

36 Remember that time in the early 1990s when it seemed like every new product was clear? There was clear beer, clear mascara, clear deodorant—*Saturday Night Live* even did a spoof commercial for clear gravy. But the most publicized clear product was Pepsi's transparent cola. It was launched with glitzy ads during the 1993 Super Bowl—and just a short time later, it was "cleared" from store shelves forever. What was this soda called?

(a) Pepsi Free

(b) Crystal Pepsi

(c) Pepsi Clear

36

(b) One noted marketing expert ranked Crystal Pepsi as the dumbest food product ever foisted on the American public. We'd say it clearly deserves an Edsel Award.

37 It seems like every year there's a new doll that every kid has to have. In fact, the buying frenzies for these dolls have become the stuff of legend. Innocent toys like Cabbage Patch Kids, Tickle Me Elmo, and Furbies have sparked near riots in toy stores. But in 1956—the year before the Edsel premiered—the Ideal Toy Company introduced a new doll that was a complete failure. What was it?

(a) The Baby Jesus Doll

(b) Wendy the Bed Wetter

(c) The Hitler Action Figure

(d) The "I Like Ike" Doll

37

(a) The Baby Jesus Doll. It came packed in a bed of straw inside a box that resembled a Bible, complete with illustrated figures of the rest of the Holy Family. Eventually Ideal took back all the unsold dolls, and tried giving them away—I guess they just couldn't bring themselves to mark down Jesus.

38 McDonald's is one of the great American success stories, but that doesn't mean the company hasn't had a few spectacular flops along the way. In 1962, McDonald's introduced a new product that failed so badly it has been called—you guessed it—the Edsel of the fast-food industry. What was this fast food called?

(a) McChicken Soup

(b) The Hula Burger

(c) McFlounder Fries

(d) The Prune Shake

38

ANSWER

(b) And get this: There wasn't any burger in a Hula Burger! It was just a slice of pineapple with cheese on a bun, which just might have something to do with why it flopped! Hey... did somebody say McDumb?

Before the Civil War, huge locomotive engines were the marvel of the age. Which leads us to our next set of questions: You're about to read five familiar names associated with railroads—which ones are real people, and which ones are fictional?

 Our first name is Butch Cassidy— was he a real person or a fictional character?

39

He was a real person. Butch Cassidy and a gang called the Wild Bunch robbed trains throughout the West starting in the 1890s.

★ ★ ★ ★ ★ ★ ★ ★

40

Next, Casey Jones, immortalized in songs, including one from the Grateful Dead. But was Casey a real person or a fictional character?

40

He was a real person. Casey Jones was an engineer known for running trains at high speeds. He died in a head-on collision between his train and another train in 1900.

41 Our third name is Snidely Whiplash—was he a real person or a fictional character?

41

A N S W E R

He was a fictional character. Snidely Whiplash is the villain known for tying Sweet Nell to the train tracks in the Dudley Do-Right cartoons.

42 Next, how about Boxcar Willie—real
person or fictional character?

42

A N S W E R

Boxcar Willie was a real person, known to country music fans as the Singing Hobo. Boxcar died in 1999, but he sold millions of albums during his career.

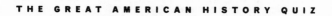

43 And finally, John Henry—was he a real person or a fictional character?

A N S W E R

Now here's an answer any politician would love: Give yourself credit for either answer. Here's why: According to legend, John Henry was a black railroad worker who battled a machine in a rock-crushing contest. John Henry won, and then died from exhaustion. But the debate over the truth of this tale has never been settled.

Our forefathers or, more probably, our foremoth-
ers used to slap laundry on a rock by the river. It
didn't actually clean the clothes very efficiently,
but it made such a pleasant sound that for years
they continued doing it. Eventually, though,
inventors devised ways to make housecleaning
faster, simpler, easier . . . and, incidentally,
lemon-scented.

 In 1874, William Blackstone made the
first of these as a birthday present for
his wife. What was it?

(a) Dishwasher

(b) Washing machine

(c) Bicycle

(d) Air conditioner

44

A N S W E R

(b) William Blackstone invented a washing machine for his wife as a birthday present in 1874. Although it's one of the world's most useful inventions, we wonder whether she wouldn't have preferred a little jewelry instead.

45 In 1946, scientist Percy L. Spencer was walking past a radar power tube, then noticed something strange: The chocolate bar in his pocket had melted. This accident led to an amazing discovery by Spencer: Microwaves generated by the radar tube had the ability to cook food. After experimenting with popcorn and eggs, Spencer developed the first commercial microwave oven, called a Radarange, which was introduced in 1947. What was the price of the first Raytheon Radarange?

(a) $30

(b) $300

(c) $3,000

45

(c) The Radarange cost $3,000 in 1947—that's equivalent to roughly $22,000 today! The first microwave ovens stood over five feet tall and weighed a whopping 750 pounds. Of course, they got a lot smaller and cheaper over time—microwave ovens are now in 90 percent of American homes.

46 The need that sparked air-conditioning was nothing less than saving the life of a U.S. president. You see, when this president was shot in 1881, it was feared he could never survive his wounds amid the heat of the Washington summer. So his room was cooled by blowing air across blocks of ice—a primitive air conditioner that worked. Name the president associated with this invention.

(a) Abraham Lincoln

(b) William McKinley

(c) James Garfield

46

(c) James Garfield. Over a half million pounds of ice were used to cool his room, but Garfield died from his wounds despite the attempts to save him.

47

Leave it to the U.S. military to turn a coffeepot into a Modern Marvel. During the 1980s the Pentagon ordered a pot that was constructed, no doubt, to exacting military specifications. And while we're certain it brewed a fine cup of coffee, the real "marvel" of this pot was its price tag. Now normally, coffeepots go for about forty bucks—how much did the Pentagon pay for theirs?

(a) $435

(b) $640

(c) $7,600

47

(c) The coffeepot cost $7,600, and who knows how much they paid for mugs? By the way, if you picked $435 or $640, you were on the right track—those were the prices paid by the Pentagon for, respectively, a hammer and a toilet seat.

Female American inventors have come a long way since Mary Kies became the first American woman to hold a U.S. patent in 1809, for her method of weaving straw with silk. Here are a few questions about female ingenuity.

 Stephanie Kwolek, a woman who, as a child, thought she might become a fashion designer, instead invented a material that would go on to save thousands of lives a year. What material, now marketed by DuPont, did she invent?

(a) Plastic

(b) Polyurethane

(c) Latex

(d) Kevlar

48

(d) Kevlar, first marketed in 1971, has been used to make bullet-proof vests, radial tires, tennis rackets, fiber-optic cables, and suits for firefighters.

49 One of the earliest pioneers of the computer revolution, she developed the computer language COBOL, the first user-friendly business software program, and was, in fact, the first person who enabled computers to "understand" commands given in the English language. Who is she?

(a) Grace Murray Hopper

(b) Frances Gabe

(c) Mae Jennison

(d) Gertrude Elion

49

(a) Grace Murray Hopper. She also reportedly coined the term "computer bug" when a moth flew into a computer processor and jammed its operation.

50 A frustrated bank secretary in the early 1950s, Bette Nesmith—the mother of Monkee Mike Nesmith—came up with an idea that would go on to help millions of secretaries, students, and executives write the perfect letter. What did she come up with?

(a) Erasers

(b) Erasable ink

(c) Liquid paper

(d) The word processor

50

(c) Liquid paper. Nesmith originally mixed liquid paper in her kitchen. Less than 15 years later, she had a factory that put out 25 million bottles of liquid paper a year!

51 One of the few female chemists working in the 1950s, Patsy Sherman, along with her colleague Sam Smith, went on to patent one of the most useful products ever invented. The idea came about when a fluoro-chemical-latex emulsion accidentally spilled onto someone's sneakers (don't you hate when that happens?). Try as they might, Patsy Sherman and her colleagues simply couldn't get the chemicals off the shoe. What invention was the result of this accident?

(a) Permanent ink

(b) Crazy Glue

(c) Scotchguard

(d) Red dye #5

ANSWER

(c) After many tests and trials, Patsy Sherman and her colleague went on to patent Scotchguard fabric protector.

52 Marion Donovan was the mother of two young daughters when she came up with this idea that would have mothers all around the world rejoicing. What did she invent?

(a) The pacifier

(b) The baby monitor

(c) The teething ring

(d) The disposable diaper

52

ANSWER

(d) Marion Donovan was the mother of the disposable diaper. First constructed out of panels from her shower curtain, Marion Donovan's Boaters, as her new product was called, were an instant hit when they went on sale in 1948. She sold her patent rights to the diaper for the remarkable sum of $1 million a short three years later.

53 Miss Anna Jarvis of Grafton, West Virginia, started wearing a white carnation and organizing special prayer sessions on a certain day every year. Before long, others began joining her, and on May 9, 1914, President Wilson signed a joint resolution of Congress to make this day a national holiday. What national holiday did Anna Jarvis "invent"?

(a) Mother's Day

(b) Father's Day

(c) Memorial Day

(d) Veterans' Day

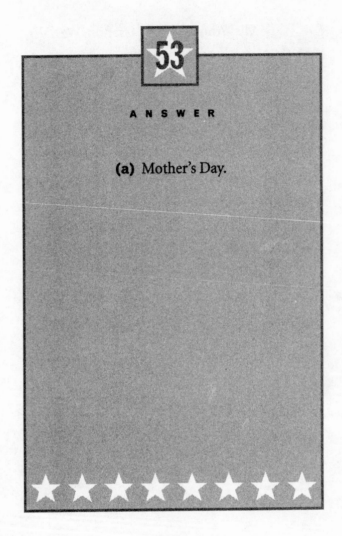

53

ANSWER

(a) Mother's Day.

It's not only the famous inventors who have created **Modern Marvels**. Did you know that Abraham Lincoln held a patent? So did Mark Twain and Hedy Lamarr. We're going to meet some tinkerers from Tinseltown. We call this category "Patents of the Rich and Famous."

 You probably never realized that some of the brightest stars in the Hollywood galaxy are also ingenious inventors. Consider those comic toasts of Tinseltown, the Marx Brothers. In 1969, a patent was granted to one brother for a special wristwatch he invented. Which brother was it?

(a) Groucho

(b) Chico

(c) Harpo

(d) Zeppo

(e) Gummo

54

(d) Zeppo. And this comedian's unique wristwatch for cardiac patients was no laughing matter. Besides keeping time, it monitored the pulse rate.

55 Of course, other celebs have followed Zeppo's path to the patent office, like the lovely Jamie Lee Curtis. The leggy star of smash-hit films is yet another rich and famous patent-holder. The question is, what did Jamie invent?

(a) A disposable garment for babies

(b) Waterproof ski gloves

(c) A sports bra

55

(a) A disposable garment for babies. Jamie herself was the baby of screen legends Tony Curtis and Janet Leigh.

★ ★ ★ ★ ★ ★ ★ ★ ★

56 Our final celebrity invention wasn't patented by a gorgeous leading lady—but the inventor is married to one! He's a rock-and-roll guitar god who holds TWO patents for guitar-related inventions. Name this inventive instrumentalist.

   (a) Duane Allman

   (b) Eddie Van Halen

   (c) Carlos Santana

56

(b) Eddie Van Halen. And when Eddie's not inventing or rocking out with his band, he's probably romancing his lovely wife, made-for-TV movie queen Valerie Bertinelli.

The story of computers goes back to the **ENIAC**, the Electronic Numerical Integrator and Computer. So how did we get from **ENIAC** to your palm-top? Let's review.

57 One year before IBM devised the first floppy disk, a California scientist named Douglas Engelbart patented the mouse, a new pointing device for computers. What year did that happen?

(a) 1963

(b) 1970

(c) 1981

57

(b) 1970. Surprisingly, Engelbart's mouse was generally not used with desktop computers for more than ten years after it was patented. Things began to change when Apple developed the Lisa computer in 1983. And one year later, the introduction of the Macintosh helped establish the mouse as an essential part of personal computers. Today, almost every house has a mouse.

58 Today's TV sets are connected to all kinds of electronics. But once upon a time, life was simpler—about the only device hooked up to a TV was a rabbit-ears antenna. Things began to change in 1972, when Magnavox introduced the world's first home videogame system—essentially a computer that plugged into a TV set. What was the system called?

(a) Odyssey

(b) Pong

(c) Intellivision

58

(a) Odyssey, which came with 12 plug-in games. That same year, 1972, Atari introduced Pong, a wildly popular computer game that changed our perception of the TV tube as a passive piece of electronics. Aaahhh...the good old days...

59 Nowadays, you'll find computer chips in everything from toasters to electric toothbrushes. Then there is the Furby, one of the most popular recent toys. Furby responds to sound, light, or touch, and he speaks about 800 phrases. How smart is Furby? Let's ask the question in terms of some other smart machines. Does Furby contain more computing power than:

(a) A Palm V Pocket Organizer

(b) A Mercedes ML320 sport utility vehicle

(c) The Apollo lunar lander

59

(c) Furby actually has more computing power than the Apollo lunar lander.

★ ★ ★ ★ ★ ★ ★ ★

Americans love cars: big cars, fast cars, leather-interiored SUVs with a CD, A/C, ABS, GPS, ABC, DEF, and GHI. But it wasn't always that way....

 Early automobiles were a rich man's luxury, but Henry Ford wanted to change that, proclaiming, "I will build a motor car for the great multitude." How he achieved that goal was a marvel all its own—Ford devised a moving assembly line to mass-produce his Model T. His assembly line allowed for a continuous flow of work, which slashed production time and dramatically lowered costs. The 1924 Model T Roadster was priced at about one third of what it had cost in 1908. Your question: What was the sticker price for a 1924 Model T Roadster?

(a) $265

(b) $950

(c) $1498

60

(a) $265, which made the Model T afford-able to the average person. At one point dur-ing its 19 years in production, more than half of all cars licensed in the U.S. were Model Ts!

61 Preston Tucker was a classic American dreamer. After World War II, he set out to design and manufacture a car that would revolutionize the auto industry. And in 1947, he rolled out the first Tucker '48 Sedan, a futuristic car with innovations like six tailpipes and a rear-mounted engine. The question is, what other feature made the Tucker an unusual car?

(a) A center headlight that turned with the steering wheel

(b) A top speed of 150 miles per hour

(c) The first fuel-injection system

61

(a) A center headlight that turned with the steering wheel. Tucker had also promised fuel injection and top speeds of 150, but couldn't deliver. And the cars he did deliver had their share of problems. Tuckers wobbled on the road and were hard to handle, and the engines were incredibly noisy. Only fifty-one cars were manufactured before Tucker went bust—but those cars sure looked fine!

62 John DeLorean was a young, fast-rising star at General Motors when he quit to start his own company and build his dream car. Dubbed the DMC-12, his slick sports car hit the market in 1981, and became a symbol of 1980s excess. Hollywood then immortalized the DeLorean by using one as a time machine in the *Back to the Future* trilogy. The question is, what metal gave the DeLorean's exterior its distinctive look?

(a) Titanium

(b) Aluminum

(c) Stainless steel

62

A N S W E R

(c) Every DeLorean had a brushed stainless steel exterior, except for two cars, which were actually gold-plated! And if you missed buying one of the roughly 8,500 DeLoreans that were built, listen up: John DeLorean is said to be developing a new car called the FireStar 500.

63 When they're not using cars, our men in uniform tool around on some two-wheelers. Which type of motorcycles did the U.S. military first use?

(a) Harley Davidson

(b) Ducati

(c) Kenilworth

(d) Excelsior-Henderson

63

ANSWER

(a) Harley Davidsons were the hogs of choice for our men in uniform.

★ ★ ★ ★ ★ ★ ★ ★

We've always thought the coolest modern marvels are the ones that fly. So please remove all metal from your pockets, and get ready for your next question. . . .

 During World War II, Nazi U-boats terrorized U.S. ships, including those carrying troops. So billionaire Howard Hughes set out to create an alternative troop transport. The result was the largest airplane ever built, with a wingspan bigger than a football field, and 50 percent larger than a 747's. The Hughes plane was called the HK-1, and nicknamed the Spruce Goose. The question is, how many times did the HK-1 fly?

(a) Once

(b) 13 times

(c) 25 times

64

A N S W E R

(a) The HK-1 was flown only once, by Howard Hughes himself. The war was over by the time the plane was finished, so it no longer had a mission. And despite its nickname, the Spruce Goose was built mainly from birch—Hughes chose to use wood for his airplane, because other materials had been needed for the war effort.

65 One look at the menacing shape of the Stealth B-2, and you know it's bad news for the enemy. Arriving without warning like some biblical plague, the B-2 bomber delivers 40,000 pounds of satellite-guided death and destruction, via conventional or nuclear payloads. One key reason for the B-2's near invisibility is that it's literally a flying wing. There's no conventional fuselage or tail, and even the engines are partly hidden inside the plane. But this unique shape posed a major problem that couldn't be solved for decades. What was it?

(a) It created a huge sonic boom

(b) There was no room to store bombs

(c) Pilots couldn't control it in flight

65

(c) Pilots couldn't control it. Although wing-shaped planes date back to the 1940s, this radar-evading design could be wildly unstable in flight. But by the time the B-2 was developed, computers were used to help pilot the plane—all this for the price of a small country.

Which came first: the chicken or the egg? You
better start thinking, because this next set of
questions falls into the category of "Which
Came First?"

66 Which came first: the discovery of
Pluto, or the debut of Goofy?

66

Astronomer Clyde Tombaugh discovered Pluto first, in 1930; two years later, Disney introduced the character who became known as Goofy.

★ ★ ★ ★ ★ ★ ★ ★ ★

67 Which came first: the first artificial heart being implanted in a human body, or hot pants as a summertime rage?

A N S W E R

The artificial heart implant was first performed in Houston, Texas, in 1969. The summer of hot pants was in 1971—that in itself was responsible for a lot of heart failures.

68 Which came first: the magnificent structure over San Francisco Bay known as the Golden Gate Bridge, or Nabisco's Oreo Cookie?

68

The Oreo, America's most popular cookie, was introduced in 1912. The Golden Gate Bridge opened in 1937, and held the title World's Longest Suspension Bridge until 1964.

69

Donald Duck, or Bugs Bunny?

69

Donald Duck. Donald debuted in 1934, while Bugs Bunny didn't spring from his wabbit hole until July 17, 1940.

70

The Frisbee, or the hula hoop?

70

A N S W E R

People began flinging the Frisbee in 1957.
The hula hoop didn't make its way around
until 1958.

71 The Hershey Chocolate Bar, or matchbooks?

A N S W E R

The Hershey Chocolate Bar came along in 1894. Matchbooks didn't catch fire until 1896.

★ ★ ★ ★ ★ ★ ★ ★ ★

The Hindenburg explosion, or the report of the disappearance of Amelia Earhart's plane during her flight over the South Pacific?

72

A N S W E R

Both of these disasters occurred in 1937. The Hindenburg went down on May 6, and Amelia Earhart's plane was reported missing on July 2.

73 The first oral contraceptive, or Mr. Potato Head?

73

Mr. Potato Head was patented in 1952. Evoid, the first oral contraceptive, was introduced in 1960, after its formulation by Frank B. Colton.

74 Thomas Edison was consumed with the business of inventing for the growing telegraph industry, often working more than 100 hours per week. His passion extended well beyond his Newark, New Jersey, laboratory. In fact, the nicknames of his first two children were telegraphic in nature. What did Edison call his kids?

(a) Mark and Space

(b) Dot and Dash

(c) AC and DC

74

(b) Thomas Jr. was called Dash, and his older sister, Marion, was Dot. Tom Jr. was a BIG problem for his father, suffering failures in businesses and marriage. He even sold the Edison name to promote quack medicines, so his father asked him to change his name. For a time, Thomas Edison, Jr., was known as Thomas Willard.

75 The next time you get a cut or a burn, you may want to thank Robert A. Chesebrough for cutting and burning himself first. You see, in the late 1800s, Chesebrough served as his own guinea pig in experiments with his new product. For weeks he gave himself small wounds to try out his invention. What was he testing?

(a) Band-Aids

(b) Bactene

(c) Vaseline

75

(c) Vaseline. Chesebrough discovered that oil field workers were treating their cuts and burns with a waxy residue that built up on their machinery. So he further developed this healing residue into what we now call Vaseline.

For the next five questions, we'll name an inventor and list four inventions. Your job is to pick the invention they are <u>not</u> associated with.

Thomas Edison:

(a) A fruit preservation method

(b) The electric chair

(c) The traffic light

(d) A device for propelling electric cars

76

ANSWER

(c) The first U.S. patent for a traffic light was issued to Garret A. Morgan in 1923. He is also credited with inventing the gas mask.

77 George Washington Carver:

(a) Bleach

(b) Buttermilk

(c) Shaving cream

(d) Drinking straws

A N S W E R

(d) Drinking straws. Although George Washington Carver was one of this country's most prolific inventors, only three patents were ever issued to him. The paper drinking straw, by the way, was patented by Marvin Stone in 1888.

78 Alexander Graham Bell:

(a) The photophone

(b) An airplane prototype

(c) The National Geographic Society

(d) Scotch Tape

78

(d) Scotch Tape was the brainchild of a 3M engineer named Richard Drew.

★ ★ ★ ★ ★ ★ ★ ★ ★

79 Benjamin Franklin:

(a) The odometer

(b) The paddle-wheel steamboat

(c) Bifocals

(d) The idea of Daylight Savings Time

79

(b) Benjamin Franklin is credited with all of these except the paddle-wheel steamboat, which was developed by Samuel Morey.

80 Nikola Tesla:

(a) The erector set

(b) The radio

(c) Neon lights

(d) The speedometer

80

(a) Though Nikola Tesla is often overlooked for his contributions to radio technology, neon lights, the speedometer, and many other inventions, he cannot take credit for the erector set. That honor goes to Alfred C. Gilbert, who debuted his product at the 1913 Toy Fair.

81 He slices, he dices, he even makes julienne fries! His name is Ron Popeil, and he's the inventor and marketing whiz behind products like the famous Veg-o-Matic. Ron launched his company, Ronco, back in the 1950s. And long before anyone ever heard the word "infomercial," Popeil was pitching his gadgets relentlessly on television. Some of his most famous successes include the Pocket Fisherman, Mr. Microphone, and a newer product called GLH Formula Number 9. Your question: What is GLH Formula Number 9?

(a) A powerful foot deodorant

(b) Fat-removing ointment

(c) Spray-on hair

81

(c) Spray-on hair. But even Popeil sometimes misses the big one—he cites the Clapper as the invention that got away, saying, "It was so simple I got mad at myself for not thinking of it."

82 Which ubiquitous household product was first introduced in 1907 to Philadelphia classrooms to prevent the spread of the common cold from child to child?

(a) Disposable paper towels

(b) Surgical masks

(c) Latex gloves

(d) Lysol

82

(a) In 1907, Scott Towels introduced the Sani-Towels Paper Towels to Philadelphia classrooms to prevent the spread of germs.

★ ★ ★ ★ ★ ★ ★ ★

83 What substance, now widely used in the making of pots and pans, did a man named Roy Plunkett discover in 1938?

(a) Aluminum

(b) Teflon

(c) Steel

83

(b) While working on a completely unre-
lated project at DuPont laboratories, Roy
Plunkett discovered Teflon, the substance
that puts the no-stick in your no-stick pots
and pans.

84 In 1907, James Spangler, a janitor in a department store in Canton, Ohio, invented the first one of these, to make his job easier:

(a) An escalator

(b) An electric vacuum cleaner

(c) A washing machine

(d) A conveyor belt

84

A N S W E R

(b) James Spangler invented the electric vacuum cleaner in 1907. Although it was originally constructed out of tin and wood, with a pillowcase for a dustbag, Spangler realized he was on to something, but didn't have the money to mass produce his invention, so he went to a childhood friend to help him out. The name of that friend? William H. Hoover.

85 Sometimes necessity is the mother of invention, but quite often it's a mother herself that's responsible. What modern medical innovation came about as a result of a young housewife's difficulties with household chores?

(a) Ben-Gay

(b) Ace bandages

(c) Band-Aids

(d) Cortisone cream

85

(c) Band-Aids. A young newlywed named Josephine Dickson would constantly get cut, burned, and banged up while keeping house. After several weeks of kitchen accidents, her husband, Earle, finally came up with the idea of attaching pieces of cotton gauze to an adhesive strip, so she could bandage herself after yet another housekeeping mishap. Hence, the Band-Aid was born.

86 An accident led to this next medical modern marvel. When trying to come up with an oscillator that would monitor the sounds of a beating heart, Wilson Greatbatch inadvertently installed a resistor with the wrong resistance into the unit, and thus stumbled onto what lifesaving device?

(a) Pacemaker

(b) Defibrillator

(c) EKG machine

(d) MRI machine

86

(a) Wilson Greatbatch invented the world's first implantable pacemaker (along with the batteries needed to run it!).

★ ★ ★ ★ ★ ★ ★ ★

87 One of the great unsung heroes of the inventing world is Walter Hunt, who is not only credited with inventing America's first sewing machine, but also with inventing the world's first safety pin. For how much did he sell the patent for the safety pin, which he invented in 1849?

(a) $400

(b) $4,000

(c) $40,000

(d) $400,000

87

ANSWER

(a) Walter Hunt thought so little of the nifty little device he came up with that he sold the patent for only $400. The reason? He wanted to pay off a $15 debt he had incurred. He also didn't patent his sewing machine, because he feared it would cause too much unemployment.

88 Sometimes public humiliation can be a good thing. When Frank MacNamara was publicly embarrassed in a New York City restaurant in 1950, he vowed never to let it happen again, so he came up with an extremely interesting idea. What did he invent?

(a) The lobster bib

(b) The calculator

(c) The cellular phone

(d) The credit card

88

ANSWER

(d) It was only after Frank MacNamara ran up a large bill entertaining guests at a restaurant that he realized he had left his wallet at home. So he and his friend Ralph Schneider came up with the Diner's Club credit card, allowing its bearers to charge food and beverages at twenty-eight participating restaurants. The first credit card in the country, Diner's Club is now welcome at over five million establishments worldwide.

89 Not only did he invent the common household wrench, one of the most useful tools in any handyman's toolbox, but African-American inventor Jack Johnson also held what remarkable title?

(a) Olympic Wrestling Champion

(b) Olympic Decathlon Athlete

(d) Second African-American to be admitted into the National Baseball League

(d) World Heavyweight Boxing Champion

89

A N S W E R

(d) The inventor of the wrench was also the first African-American to ever hold the World Heavyweight Boxing Champion title, a feat he accomplished in 1908.

90 The first public telegraph message between two cities occurred on May 24, 1844. Morse sent a message from the Supreme Court in Washington, D.C., to the Mount Clair train station in Baltimore. What message was sent?

(a) "Can you hear me, brother?"

(b) "What hath God wrought?"

(c) "America, the Beautiful"

(d) "Please send money"

90

(b) The first public telegraph message was selected from the Bible by the daughter of the commissioner of patents.

91 The first words Thomas Edison recorded on his new phonograph didn't come from as noteworthy a source as the Bible, but are nonetheless just as important. What were the first words recorded on the phonograph on November 29, 1877?

(a) "Jack and Jill"

(b) "Little Miss Muffett"

(c) "Mary Had a Little Lamb"

(d) "Twinkle, Twinkle, Little Star"

91

A N S W E R

(c) Mary and her little lamb were the subject of the first words ever recorded on the phonograph.

92 The nation's first institution of higher learning to admit women to its college programs on an equal basis with men was also the first institution to admit qualified African-Americans to its classes. What marvelous institution was this?

    (a) William and Mary

    (b) Yale

    (c) Columbia

    (d) Oberlin

92

A N S W E R

(d) Oberlin College in Oberlin, Ohio.

93 Believe it or not, it didn't happen in Texas, or in the Middle East. Where was the world's first oil well dug?

(a) Titusville, Pennsylvania

(b) Troy, New York

(c) Juneau, Alaska

(d) Tulsa, Oklahoma

93

ANSWER

(a) The world's first oil well was dug on August 28, 1859, in Titusville, Pennsylvania, by a man named Edwin L. Drake.

94 It's true what they say: The apple doesn't fall far from the tree. What ingenious toy was invented by the son of famous architect Frank Lloyd Wright?

(a) Lincoln Logs

(b) Lego

(c) The erector set

(d) Waffle Blocks

94

A N S W E R

(a) John Wright got the idea for inventing Lincoln Logs by watching his father work on the Imperial Hotel in Tokyo.

Our last category: "Space, the Final Frontier."
Space travel may be the greatest marvel of the
twentieth century. In any case, **NASA** technology has led to some marvelous inventions. Your
job right now is to decide whether the following
products are **NASA or NOT.**

 The uses for Teflon range from cook-
ware to lubrication. But was Teflon
created for NASA or NOT?

95

The answer is NOT. A DuPont chemist accidentally discovered Teflon in 1938. Didn't you read question 83?

96 Next, the ever handy and helpful Dustbuster vacuum. Did this invention result from NASA technology or NOT?

96

The answer is NASA. Black and Decker developed the Dustbuster, basing it on the motor for a cordless drill they had designed for NASA.

97 Quartz watches and clocks are now the standard for telling time. Is the quartz clock NASA or NOT?

97

ANSWER

The answer is NASA—quartz clocks origi-
nated with the Apollo missions.

98 The next product is Tang breakfast drink—was this famous orange powder invented for NASA or NOT?

98

The answer is NOT. Although well known for its use in the space program, Tang debuted as a civilian drink in 1959.

Here are a few more questions about the last frontier.

 Which astronaut was not on *Apollo 11*?

(a) Michael Collins

(b) Buzz Aldrin

(c) Walter Cunningham

99

(c) Walter Cunningham was not on board *Apollo 11*. He was the lunar module pilot for *Apollo 7*.

100 Which nickname was given to the Apollo mission simulator?

(a) The Speeding Bullet

(b) The Space Coaster

(c) The Train Wreck

(d) The Challenger

ANSWER

(c) The Train Wreck. Apparently training on the Apollo mission simulator was not the most pleasant way to spend a Sunday afternoon.

101 Which type of container was used to hold the pureed food of early space flights?

(a) A Ziplock bag

(b) A shampoo bottle

(c) A mustard squirter

(d) A toothpaste container

A N S W E R

(d) Toothpaste containers originally held all of the pureed food on the early space flights.